The Story of *Mary* the Mother of God

Dorrie Papademetriou

ST. VLADIMIR'S SEMINARY PRESS
2000

For my mother and father

The publication of this book was
made possible in part due to the generosity of
Mr. & Mrs. Mark Hudoff.

Dorrie Papademetriou is a graphic designer and artist. She received a
Bachelor of Fine Arts from Bowling Green State University. Her work
is inspired by her travels through Greece and Turkey, where she studied
the colors, the light, as well as the faith and traditions of the people.
She lives with her husband and two young sons in Princeton, NJ.

PRINTED IN HONG KONG

A Note about the Story

Most of us know who the Virgin Mary is either spiritually, visually, or intellectually. In each of these encounters, we tend to know Mary mostly as the mother and bearer of God (*Theotokos*) in the person of His Son, Jesus Christ. Although I was always aware of the importance of the Virgin Mary, it was through depictions of her early life that I felt for the first time I could understand who she was and why she was chosen by God to be a "bridge between heaven and earth."

While I was living in Istanbul, Turkey in 1998, I visited the Monastery of Chora (Kariye Djami) which is one of the marvelous Byzantine treasures of that city. High in the domes of the inner narthex of this 14th century church, I witnessed an amazing sequence of mosaics that depicted the early life of the Virgin Mary.

In retelling her wonderful story, I depend on these mosaic icons as well as on various ancient texts and legends, much of which make up the tradition of the Church. Although the Bible gives very little information about Mary, texts not officially accepted by the Church, such as the Apocryphal Gospel of St. James (Protoevangelium), offer more detailed stories of her early life. I have used these materials to present a story of Mary that I hope will lead to a greater understanding of who the person of Mary is.

–Dorrie Papademetriou

Many years ago in the land of Nazareth lived a husband and wife, Joachim and Anna, who had been blessed by God with many good things. The lived happily in a beautiful home, with fine clothes, and plenty to eat. But as they grew older, what they wanted more than anything in the world was to share their love with a child of their own.

On the great day of the Lord, all the people would go to the Temple to make offerings to God for thanksgiving and forgiveness. Joachim and Anna filled their carts with oil, wheat, grapes, fresh vegetables, sheep, milk, and cheeses to make their own offerings. As they approached the Temple with all their gifts, the high priest Zacharias saw them and raised his hand to tell them to stop. Surprised and stunned, Joachim and Anna wondered why their gifts were not accepted. They learned that it was because they had no children; it was not lawful for them to offer gifts.

Both Joachim and Anna felt terrible and very sad. Joachim decided to go far away into the wilderness to pray. There he pitched his tent among the rocks and trees and prayed to God for a child for 40 days and 40 nights.

While Joachim was away, Anna went walking in her garden. As she looked up, she saw a nest of baby sparrows in a laurel tree. The mother was caring for her baby birds. Tears filled Anna's eyes because she had no children of her own to care for. Her heart was heavy and she prayed to God for a child.

Just then an angel came to Anna and said, "Anna, Anna the Lord has heard your prayer. You will have a child and she will be famous in all the world." Anna said to the angel, "My child will be a gift to God and she will serve Him all the days of her life." At the same time an angel came to Joachim and said, "Joachim, Joachim, the Lord has heard your prayer..."

When Anna saw Joachim returning from the wilderness she was so happy she ran to him and threw her arms around his neck and told him about the angel she saw. Smiling, she said, "Now I know the Lord has greatly blessed me."

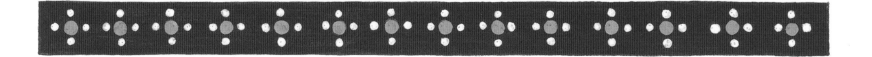

Months passed and a beautiful baby girl was born. Anna was filled with great love for her new baby. She called her Mary. When Anna held Mary, she remembered the mother and baby birds. Now she had her own baby to care for and she was very happy.

Day by day Mary grew into a beautiful little girl. When she was six months old her mother would sit close and play with her. Once while they played Anna placed her on the carpet among the soft pillows. With outstretched hands the tiny baby Mary walked her first seven steps.

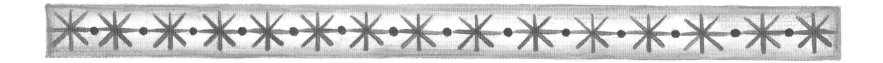

Joachim, Anna, and Mary lived happily and shared much joy. Their hearts were full of love.

Mary sang songs unto the Lord. When she was three years old, her mother and father walked with her and presented her to the Temple. The high priest kissed her and blessed her and sat her on the third step of the altar. Joachim and Anna marveled at Mary as she twirled and danced about happily. And all the house of Israel loved her.

Mary was special. Because she was so special, an angel would come visit Mary in the Temple. The angel placed bread in her hand for her to eat.

The priests of the council loved Mary very much. They met to decide what would be best for her. Zacharias, the high priest, took his robe with the twelve bells and went to the altar to pray concerning Mary. An angel came to Zacharias and said, "Gather all the good men and let each one bring a staff to the Temple. Whoever receives a sign from the Lord will be the husband of Mary." As the line of men neared the end, there was still no sign. Finally, Joseph, who was last in line, came forward and placed his staff before Zacharias and everyone was amazed as it sprouted forth flowers and green leaves, and at the same time a dove flew upon his head. Joseph was to be the husband of Mary.

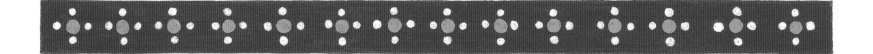

Mary and Joseph walked down the long road to his home where he would look after her.

The priests of the Temple were very happy for her and satisfied that she was well cared for by Joseph. When it came time to weave a new veil for the Temple of the Lord, they asked Mary to weave the royal colors, the true purple and scarlet. Mary set right to work weaving the most special cloth for the Temple.

Mary worked with great care as she weaved the cloth of true purple and scarlet. After some time, she became thirsty and went to the well to draw some water. As she filled the pitcher, the great archangel Gabriel appeared to her and said, "Rejoice, Mary full of grace, the Lord is with you; Blessed are you among women."

When Mary heard this she grew worried wondering what Gabriel meant. And Gabriel said, "Do not be afraid Mary, for God loves you very much. And behold, you will bring forth in your womb a son and shall call his name Jesus. He will be great, and will be called the Son of the Highest and the Lord God will give him the throne of his forefather David, and he will reign over the house of Jacob forever, and of his kingdom there will be no end." And Mary said, "Behold, I am the maidservant of the Lord! Let it be according to your word." When the archangel Gabriel departed, Mary returned to her home to finish weaving the cloth for the Temple.

Throughout her life, Mary walked in the Light of God. Because of her great faith and devotion she became the Mother of God, the Theotokos, and she marvelled at her Son Jesus all the days of her life.